# The City of Carcassonne

## W9-CDY-440

In July 1928, the citizens of Carcassonne celebrated the city's bimillennium. Presided over by Gaston Doumergue, President of the Republic, this rather pompous ceremony marked the result of a century of combats which witnessed the evolution of the city's fortifications from insalubrious ruins to historic monument. With restorations completed in 1910, tourist activity increased between the wars, initially reserved for a wealthy elite, but soon democratised. Designated a UNESCO world heritage site, the city now receives approximately two million visitors annually.

Carcassonne citizens well understood the City's new vocation—henceforth a kind of stone book inscribed with local history—yet in 1928 modestly shied away from attributing an exact date to their city's birth, which remained somewhat arbitrary.

Tour de la Justice, west facade, and Counts' château.

1

# HISTORY

## The oppidum

Archeological evidence points to the fact that by the late 8th century B.C., an agglomeration suggesting both a "rough sketch of a city" and a place of exchange had developed on the site of Carcas, two kilometres south-west of the actual City of Carcassonne. Carsac might possibly be considered ancestor to the Carcaso oppidum which likely had been established around mid-6th century B.C. Like many oppidums (or *oppida*), small villages perched on a hill, Carcaso would have been fortified. Preoccupation for security partially explains the choice of a rocky spur naturally protected by northern and western slopes, but also a desire, perhaps more important, to ensure the ability to survey and thus control a space destined originally for movement of men and goods.

At the continental scale, the Narbonne-Bordeaux axis (in which Carcassonne was one of the milestones) remained the shortest overland route between the Mediterranean and the Atlantic. On a regional scale, the straight corridor between Corbières and Montagne Noire (which overlooks Carcassonne) constituted

West facade on the steepest slope of the City.

the easiest route from the sea toward Toulouse and Aquitaine. Locally, the City (which dominates the Aude River by some fifty metres, not far from the point of the river's eastward deviation) commanded a crossroad at which two routes of lesser importance converged, perpendicular to the previously discussed grand east-west axis. The southerly route followed the upper Aude Valley and led to the Pyrenees hills opening up toward roads to Spain. The northerly route gravitated toward the Montagne Noire slopes into the heart of the Massif Central, bordering a mining zone (iron, copper, silver lead, gold) exploited from at least the 1st century B.C. Numerous Etruscan, Punic, and Greek pottery shards excavated in the City confirm the role of the Carcaso oppidum as a resting station along the route to Aquitaine.

From the 3rd century B.C., Campanian-style ceramics appeared more and more frequently as Roman commercial dominance imposed itself, especially over the wine trade. In this manner, merchants preceded Domitius Aenobarbus' legionnaires, who easily conquered southern Gaul in 118 B.C.

## The Roman city

The importance of the Roman city of Carcaso is difficult to evaluate. Described as an *oppida latina*, it became a county town of the *colonia Julia Carcaso* by the last quarter of the 1st century B.C. The city was an administrative centre, but what of its economic strength and influence between the two poles of Narbonne and Toulouse? In Carcassonne, several vestiges of dwellings have been excavated. Walls are covered in rose-coloured plaster, and flooring sometimes composed of rather simple white mosaic with black motifs, indicating a comfortable, rather than luxurious, living standard. At the northern foothill extended a rather vast area in which constructions and silos followed in sequence along the route to Aquitaine, perhaps as far as the banks of the Aude.

In 333 A.D., the itinerary of a pilgrimage from Bordeaux to Jerusalem mentions the Carcassonne *castellum* in a list of milestones including inns, post houses, markets, and county towns of the city. Carcassonne was no longer a *civitas* like Narbonne, probably a sign of a certain decline during a period in which large rural estates had developed. What

is the derivation of the word *castellum*? Little doubt remains of the existence of a fortified enclosure encircling the urban core established at the hill summit. Very numerous, extant vestiges of this enclosure served as a skeleton for the present interior rampart.

Vestiges of the Gallo-Roman rampart set back from the late 13th-century interior rampart, between the Tour du Trésau and Tour du Moulin du Connétable, seen from the northern front.

The Gallo-Roman enclosure encompassed a surface of just over seven hectares. Its construction came within the framework of a general movement to enclose towns within protective ramparts against the first waves of foreign invasions.

But it was only a century later that the City began to fulfil the strategic role which would mark its history for more than a millennium, since he who held control of the City controlled lower Languedoc.

Porte de Rodez, between the Tour de la Marquière and Tour de Samson on the northern front of the late-Empire interior enclosure, overlooking the lower lists.

# Between Franks and Visigoths

In the early 5th century, the City was part of the southern fringe of Gaul held by the Roman Empire. But the Visigoths installed in Aquitaine forced the wedge which gave them access to the route to Spain. In 507, the Franks drove the Visigoths out of Aquitaine; however the latter held onto lower Languedoc (then called Septimanie or Gothie) and came to dominate the major part of the Iberian peninsula. From 508, Clovis unsuccessfully attacked Carcassonne, which had blocked Frankish expansion toward the Mediterranean shores. In 585, the city was again besieged, this time successfully, but the Visigoths recovered it shortly thereafter. Arab conquest of Spain marked the demise of the Visigoth realm. The City appears to have resisted an initial raid in the early 8th century. In 725, it was besieged and captured, but Arab occupation lasted briefly, and from the mid-8th century, Septimanie was conquered by Pépin the Short.

## The first counts

Between Aquitaine and Septimanie, the county of Carcassonne (granted to Goths issued from a family who had participated in the struggle against the Arabs) impeded the establishment of a vast southern entity which eluded Carolingian power. Therefore the first counts Bellon and Oliba II were the object of the Emperor's specific solicitude, followed by that of King Charles the Bald in the context of *Francia Occidentalis*. Due to the absence of a direct heir, this first dynasty died out in approximately the mid-10th century. It was replaced by a new line of counts originating from the Pyrenees region of Comminges and Couserans, in its turn expiring with the last representative, Roger III, who died without issue. In 1067, the Carcassès and Razès were to enlarge the estates of Roger III's sister Ermengarde, Viscountess of Agde and Béziers, and wife of Raimond Bernard Trencavel, Viscount of Albi and Nîmes.

Detail of the mural painting embellishing the circular room of the Counts' château, illustrating a battle between Franks and Saracens.

It seems that the couple scarcely managed to hold onto their inheritance: the following year, for a very large sum of gold, they sold "the city of Carcassonne and its villages" to Raimond Berganger I (d. 1076), Count of Barcelona, accepting his suzerainty over Carcassès and Razès.

In 1082, Raimond Berganger II was assassinated by his twin brother in Carcassonne. Bernard Aton (Ermengarde and Raimond Bernard Trencavel's son) immediately invested the city, proclaiming himself its defendant during the minority of the defunct count's heir. Nine years later, he refused to render the city to its legitimate owner.

Marble sarcophagus with wheat-sheaf and vine motifs from Floure (Aude), Merovingian period (Carcassonne, lapidary deposit, Château comtal).

## Between Barcelona and Toulouse

By his usurpation and unremitting effort to possess the city, Bernard Aton transformed Carcassonne into the keystone of a group of strongholds which, in the wake of estate divisions, was reduced or reconstituted, but remained sufficiently powerful to thwart ambitious moves from Barcelona and Toulouse. In 1107,

Tour du Moulin d'Avar postern on the northern front of the late-Empire enclosure.

Carcassonne inhabitants (who scarcely tolerated the Trencavels' brutal greed) called upon the Count of Barcelona for the first time, swearing allegiance to him and chasing Bernard Aton out of the city. With the Count of Toulouse's assistance, Aton recaptured the city. In 1112, Raimond Berganger III headed for Carcassonne with a strong army; Trencavel raised the troop. It required the Archbishop of Narbonne's intervention to prevent actual confrontation. In 1120, a new revolt of Carcassonne and regional lords put Bernard Aton into a difficult position. He reinstated his authority four years later, with the backing of the Count of Toulouse. In this way, during a preliminary phase enduring from 1082 to 1124, Bernard Aton's obstinacy blocked Catalan expansionism. The following years marked a change

## The Cathars

Questions on the sorrow and salvation of souls were the focus of reflection of those who claimed the title "the poor of Christ" and whom their sympathizers dubbed the "bonshommes" [good-natured souls]. Today they are referred to as "Cathars", meaning the 'pure' or 'perfect'.

According to the Cathars, the visible, carnal world where evil is omnipresent could not be the work of God who, in essence, is infinitely good. Salvation cannot come except by a total detachment from the world created by Satan. Such is what Christ, assuming a human appearance, came to announce.

The "bonshommes" repudiate Incarnation, Resurrection, and the Last Judgement. Hell is already on earth, all souls shall be saved, but their sojourn in the evil world will endure as long as they do not observe the Evangelical message as interpreted by those who believe themselves to be the "Apostles of Christ". That message calls for chastity, humility, frequent prayer, fasting, refusal of homicide, theft, and falsehood, abstinence from all animal foods, acceptance of death as deliverance … All symbols like the cross and all images are rejected as descending from an evil world. Only the *consolamentum*, the last rite transmitted through the laying on of hands, brings the spirit to truth and salvation, its passage to the other world, eternal, incorruptible, and invisible, where God reigns.

Giving great importance to those passages in the Gospels which conform to their concepts—in the Lord's Prayer, for example, they lay stress on the expression "deliver us from evil"—Cathars claim themselves to be "good Christians". Opposed to the Catholic Church, which they consider rooted in the temporal, they developed a separate church with its own bishops and religious communities.

in alliances. Since Raymond IV, the Toulousian counts had been manoeuvering to extend their authority from the Garonne to the Rhône. Confronted by this threat, it seems that the Trencavels chose the Catalan camp, whose power increased in 1137 with the union of the Houses of Aragon and Barcelona. These fickle alliances and independence vis-à-vis two political powers which, from the 12th century, claimed to federate Languedoc, resulted in isolating the Trencavels just when it was necessary to withstand the impact of the Crusade.

## The eve of the Crusade

By the early 13th century, the late-Empire enclosure encircled the City only. The fortification dated back nine centuries, yet had not become obsolete. Since Bernard Aton, defence had been confined to the knights who had a house at their disposal

Tour du Moulin du Connétable, Tour du Vieulas and Tour de la Marquière, on the interior enclosure, which reiterate late-Empire features.

Interior enclosure bond* detail, dating from the late-Empire (here largely restored).

*Terms followed by an asterisk are explained in the glossary at the end of the book.

within the City and earned their revenue from a few neighbouring estates. The first Carcassonne counts appear to have occupied the "Narbonne Château", of which no vestiges remain, but whose name suggests that the building was situated near the city entry.

From this most exposed site, the seigneurial estate was transferred to the summit of the hill, probably a few years after Bernard Aton's death. Charters designate this new building as the *palatium*. It was undoubtedly a fortified residence conceived in the same spirit as those which housed the lords in close proximity to the local population at the centre of the Languedoc *castra*.

The town prospered. It housed around three to four thousand persons scattered within several distinct agglomerations. In fact, the City was flanked by two market towns. Surviving from the Roman period, the northern village likely became more densely populated, its constructions approaching ever closer to the Gallo-Roman enclosure despite the steep slope. It acquired the name *bourg* [market town

or village] Saint-Vincent. Perhaps during the Carolingian period, the village of Saint-Michel grew to the south and east which, from the Porte Narbonnaise to the east, covered an area stretching beyond the City's southern gate.

*The Pope excommunicating the Albigensians* and *Massacre of the Albigensians,* miniatures from *Chronicles of Saint-Denis,* second quarter of the 14th century (London, British Library).

Like Saint-Michel, the town of Saint-Vincent was encircled by a trench and rampart abutting the City enclosure.

In 1209, Viscount Raimond Roger Trencavel turned twenty-four years old. It appears that he was a good Catholic, although his parents received both Christians and Cathars on equal footing in their castle, and his main advisor, Roger de Cabaret, was a notorious follower of dualist theories. With Albi and Toulouse, Carcassonne incontestably formed a triangle where heresy thrived. On Trencavel lands, the average bloke was not in the least anxious.

## The "exhibition of remorse"

In response to Innocent III, the Crusaders carried out their mission to dispossess those lords who tolerated heresy. Their expedition turned against Raimond Roger Trencavel: his lands were "exhibited in remorse" and offered to the Crusaders. They followed the Rhône Valley and arrived first at Béziers. Trencavel withdrew to Carcassonne. This choice confirms the importance that the viscounts accorded to the town, and the confidence inspired by the City's Gallo-Roman fortifications with their three-metre-thick ramparts and at least thirty-four flanking towers. Béziers was rapidly captured following an unfortunate departure of its defenders, its population massacred, and the city set on fire. On 28 July 1209, the Crusaders took up position before Carcassonne. On 15 August, Trencavel gave himself up in order to obtain safety for the inhabitants in return for renouncement of all their belongings and exodus to neighbouring villages. The northern town had already been captured on the first day of August, the southern town a week later. Conquering the City defences undoubtedly would have demanded much more time, but a multitude of reasons pleaded in favour of surrender. Firstly, there

## Crusade against the Albigensians

The Crusade responded both to a failure and an inadequacy.

Failure was that of preaching, despite the Dominicans' persuasive efforts and their willingness to set an example of poverty similar to that of the "bonshommes".

Inadequacy was that of the Provençal lords whom the Church awaited to pursue heretics. However, as many of them had converted to dualism, becoming indifferent or motivated by strong anticlericalism widespread amongst Languedoc nobles, the Midi lords did not play the role of "secular arm".

In 1208, Pope Innocent III appealed to the Crusade. This period can be divided into three schematic phases.

The **first** phase corresponds to the 1209 military expedition which reunited European barons, the majority northern French, against those commonly called "Albigensians", even though the city of Albi does not appear to have played any more significant a role than any other city in the spread of heresy. Once Raymond VI of Toulouse was subjugated, the Crusaders targeted Raimond Roger Trencavel, Viscount of Carcassonne, as their principal adversary. After the sack and conflagration of Béziers, Trencavel, isolated in the City, gave himself up on 15 August 1209. One of the Crusader lords, Simon de Montfort, became the new Viscount of Carcassonne.

The **second** phase related to the merciless struggle led by Montfort and several companions against the Albigensians and local lords who refused his suzerainty. Montfort's ambition and Raymond VI of Toulouse's abrupt reversals enlarged the whole of Languedoc with land disputed between Crusaders and Midi lords.

The **third** phase involved the King of France's intervention. After Montfort's death in 1218, faced with the difficulty of holding onto the region, his son Amaury renounced rights over Trencavel's lands. In 1224 he ceded them to the King, who took charge of a major new military expedition. In 1226, the campaign was consecrated to the annexation of a major part of Languedoc to the royal domain. With the 1229 Treaty of Paris, Raymond VII of Toulouse wed his daughter to young King Louis IX's brother, thus opening up the possibility (later realized) of Toulouse's unification with the Crown.

By a concurrence of circumstances, the Crusade against the Albigensians entered into the slow process of unification of the realm.

Stone of the Siege, perhaps an illustration of one of the episodes in the Albigensian Crusade; located in the south transept arm of Saint-Nazaire Basilica.

was the disequilibrium of forces—the combined strength of the Crusaders' army, including both knights and villagers, probably added up to a few thousand, while Trencavel's forces numbered a few hundred. Secondly, Peter II of Aragon's mediation had failed, and the King of Aragon refused to engage himself with a vassal who several times had been formally ordered to prosecute heretics. Thirdly, living conditions in the City were arduous: Crusaders controlled all access to the Aude River and the Fontgrande spring south of the city, whilst provision of well and cistern water in the August heat proved insufficient with the influx of refugees from the market towns. Lastly, the psychological shock of the Béziers massacre was doubtlessly the determining factor. The Crusaders' determination to terminate as quickly as possible, having at their disposal a city intact and sizeable plunder, ended with a transaction in which Raimond Roger paid dearly.

None of the great lords who participated in the Crusades wanted Roger's lands. They chose as new viscount Simon de Montfort, a minor lord from the Île-de-France known for his courage and piety. Whilst imprisoned, Raimond Roger died on 10 November 1209, leaving his two-year-old son entrusted to the Count of Foix. At the same moment, the Pope confirmed Montfort in his new fiefs. Once again it became necessary to submit or dispossess the lords of the *castra* and mountain châteaux which had protected heretics. Montfort acted with brutal efficiency, installing his companions onto conquered fiefs.

# Annexation of the royal domain

In 1211, Simon de Montfort attacked the remaining territories of the Count of Toulouse. In 1213, the Battle of Muret ended with the flight of Raymond VI's troops and the death of Peter II of Aragon, who had come to support him. A model Catholic but suzerain to the Viscount of Carcassonne, arrogantly snubbed by Montfort who solely recognized the King of France as his master, Peter II had resumed the same policy of interventionism beyond the Pyrenees which his ancestors had conducted. Muret had de facto severed ties between Carcassonne and Aragon. In 1218, Montfort died outside of Toulouse; his body was brought back to the City, and buried for a time in Saint-Nazaire Cathedral. In 1224, his son Amaury returned to the Île-de-France,

Fleur-de-lys blazon of the Seneschalsy of Carcassonne, stoneware, 14th century (Carcassonne, lapidary deposit, Château comtal).

having ceded his rights over the Midi to Louis VIII. In 1226, heading a powerful army, the King of France took possession of lands which had reverted to him. Just as royal troops were approaching Avignon, Carcassonne consuls handed over the keys of the City to Louis VIII. The city was selected as headquarters of a seneschal's court, a centre of incitement from which the royal administration established itself over the whole of western Languedoc. The city also experienced another change in becoming an impressive fortified town.

## The fortified town

During the last two-thirds of the 13th century, large-scale building works drastically changed the appearance of the City in response to several objectives: to assure the security of the King's men in an environment still largely hostile; to impede all attempts to recapture the city while Raimond Trencavel (heir to the dynasty refuged in Aragon) refused to renounce the lands he considered his spoils; to meet any eventual return of Aragon expansionism; and lastly, in a general manner, to sway the spirit of the populations, feudal and princely, with the execution of major building works that a simple lord would have been incapable of carrying off. The majority of such

East facade enclosure, Counts' château; from right to left, Tour du Major, Tour des Casernes, Tour de la Porte de l'Est, and Tour Saint-Paul.

works carried the imprimatura of royal architects, testifying to a novel concept of defence that had developed since Philip Augustus's reign. Ramparts and towers no longer had a simple protective function, nor one of refuge from eventual limited reprisals; construction became auxiliary to active defence, with an emphasis on inflicting adversarial losses.

The first building campaign, which most likely was launched just after annexation, involved the château. The Trencavels' *palatium* buildings, abutting the Gallo-Roman fortification wall at the western summit of the hill, were surrounded on the remaining three sides by a rampart flanked by towers which completely isolated them from the town, thereby assuring protection of the King's representatives against a population whose fidelity remained dubious. As the first building phase terminated, a second enclosure was erected in subsequent years in front of the Gallo-Roman rampart, reinforced by fourteen towers for a perimetre of only some one and a half kilometres. The enclosure appeared more as a primary obstacle to hinder all attempted assaults or sapping, rather than as a work of elaborate defence. On the western front, a covered path was installed which allowed safe descent of the hill's very steep slope. It subsequently terminated with a wide barbican*, a jutting construction which controlled the banks of the Aude. This was doubtless the state of City defences when, in 1240, it underwent the last siege in its history.

On 17 September 1240, arriving from Aragon to rejoin several lords equally dispossessed, Raimond Trencavel was greeted as liberator by the townspeople. The assaults he launched on the City's double enclosures and on the Aude Barbican, as well as the galleries of pits dug from the townhouses, threatened the remarkable defence organised by Seneschal Guillaume des Ormes. On 11 October, while royal reinforcements were advancing, Trencavel and his partisans raised the siege. Before

South wall of the Counts' château enclosure. The window illuminated the ceremonial hall which stood in the present Midi Court; at right, the Tour Saint-Paul.

*Following pages*

Western front of the interior enclosure with, from left to right, the Counts' château, Tour de la Justice, and Porte d'Aude.

Louis IX, he solemnly renounced his rights to Carcassonne in 1247.

The day after the 1240 siege, abandoned towns were destroyed and the exterior enclosure repaired and completed by fine creations like the Tour de la Vade and the Tour de la Peyre. The upper northern and western sections of the Gallo-Roman enclosure were rebuilt. From the rather distinct terracing work, the lists partially levelled off. The château buildings received additional storeys and, in place of the actual Midi Court, a vast, ceremonial hall supported by piers was fitted out. Lastly, between the château and the city's western Porte d'Aude, the Tour de la Justice was erected.

A final construction campaign was extended during Philip the Bold's last reigning years (1270-1285) through to Philip the Fair's first years (1285-1314). This activity was perhaps related to mounting tension between France and Aragon after 1280, linked to intrigues of Charles I d'Anjou, uncle to the King of France. The entire south corner of the interior enclosure was reconstructed. On the eastern front, the late-Empire rampart and towers served as core to a more elaborate fortification. Ultimately the impressive, unified design from the Porte Narbonnaise to the Tour du Trésau and high rampart to the north constituted the termination of a series of reconstructions and improvements which made the late 13th-century City a "master fortress" (as Charles VI would still qualify it one century later).

Drawbridge reconstituted on the exterior enclosure, with the Tours de la Porte Narbonnaise and Tour du Trésau of the interior enclosure.

# Attack and defence

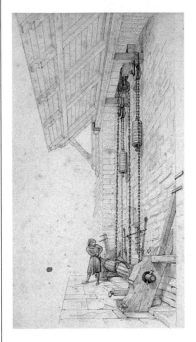

Defense systems are responses to different assault techniques in as much as the progress of those techniques lead to the amelioration of those defences.

To penetrate a city, it was necessary either to scale the walls, or to make one or several breaches in them.

Easy to put into operation, scaling had limited chances of success because ladders, if there was not an element of surprise, could be readily pushed out of the way. Assailants often constructed mobile wooden towers, sometimes called "beffrois" [belfries], that were pushed against the ramparts. The approach of these belfries was impeded by the trenches, although at Carcassonne, as in very many other fortifications, they never contained water.

Sappers and miners attempted to collapse the wall by digging (either beneath or at its base) a cavity which they progressively shored up. Then, fire set to the props caused the collapse of the bare wall which was no longer supported. Medieval artillery (*trébuchets* or "bird-traps", *mangonneaux* or "mangona") aimed at destroying the crenellations and roofs in order to expose their defenders.

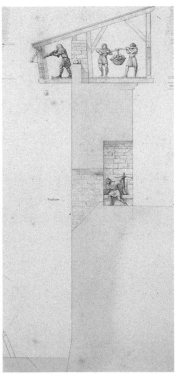

View of the mechanism of the Porte Narbonnaise's second portcullis, and section through the curtain wall furnished with wooden trestle within the Tour du Trésau; ink drawings with gouache heightening by Eugène Viollet-le-Duc, 1853 (Paris, MAP).

# Carcassonne's dual destiny

With the 1258 Treaty of Corbeil, Louis IX brought the law in accordance with events. He renounced the suzerainty that the Kings of France, since Charlemagne's conquests, had claimed to exercise over Roussillon and Catalonia. In exchange, the King of Aragon himself renounced those Languedoc lands which he held by right of homage.

On home ground, the treaty had been prepared by putting into place a network of fortifications which left no doubt regarding the limits of the kingdom that Louis IX intended to establish. On the crest of the high Corbières mountains separating France and Aragon, the châteaux of Puylaurens, Aguilar, Quéribus, Peyrepertuse, and Termes simultaneously served as advance posts, surveillance points, and signals of intimidation. Set back, the City functioned as a border town, strengthened by a garrison of two hundred and twenty sergeants and an impressive arms-and-war materials depot. It was at the moment when the City's military vocation thus reached its height that the lower town was created. By the mid-13th century, a vast territory on the left bank of the Aude was conceded to the inhabitants of the old towns. The new city adopted a rigorous grid pattern of streets and plots typical of walled towns, which were multiplying during this period. The two market towns sprang to life again

The 13th-century City and lower town, ink drawing by Jean-Claude Golvin (*Carcassonne. Le temps des sièges*, 1992).

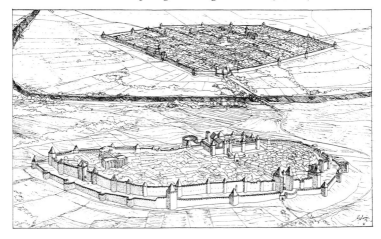

The City and lower town today.

as two parishes, Saint-Vincent to the north, and Saint-Michel to the south. The lower town rapidly prospered as a result of the drapery industry, but the City languished due to a lack of any ostensible threat to its border. In 1418, the garrison was reduced by half, service having become hereditary which, despite several constraints, allowed soldiers to exercise a second trade.

The 1659 Treaty of the Pyrenees definitively incorporated Roussillon as part of France and shifted the border toward the Pyrenees summits. The City's strategic role faded away. The sole danger threatening it at this point was the prosperity of the lower town, attracting to it magistrates, royal officers, ecclesiastics, and the like.

At the beginning of the 19th century, the City was no more than a poor district housing the most impoverished weavers, as outlets for the clothing industry in the direction of the Levant closed down, stifling the dynamism of merchants and fabric manufacturers. Still proprietor of the fortifications, the army was ready to deliver them up to the demolishers' axe. Only energetic intervention by Carcassonne's Jean-Pierre Cros-Mayrevieille, with the help of Prosper Mérimée, narrowly saved both towers and ramparts. Local scholars Mérimée and Eugène Viollet-le-Duc made the great majority of people aware of the fact that the City fortifications constituted "a unique ensemble and the most remarkable model of medieval military architecture" (Viollet-le-Duc).

# Chronology

Establishment of a chronology, particularly concerning the fortifications, suffers from a paucity of sources. Marginal notes and dates proposed here—or resumption of work led by archeologists and historians—are the result of a collation of interpretations of known texts, an analysis of the historical context, and a comparison with other examples of military architecture. As a consequence, information is not irrefutable.

**Early 7th century-mid-6th century B.C.** Occupation of the site of Carsac.

**Mid-6th century B.C.** First traces of the occupation of the City site.

**118 B.C.** Roman conquest of southern Gaul.

**333 B.C.** Carcaso is designated as a *castellum*.

**507** Chased out of Aquitaine by the Franks, the Visigoths maintain hold over lower Languedoc.

**725** Beginning of a short-lived Saracen occupation.

**1082** Bernard Aton Trencavel proclaims himself Viscount of Carcassonne.

**1096** Construction of Saint-Nazaire Cathedral begins.

**Between 1120 and 1150** Trencavels' *palatium* construction.

**1209** Crusade against the Albigensians, capture of Carcassonne, and Simon de Montfort's ascension as new viscount.

**1226** Annexation of Carcassonne to the royal domain.

**Circa 1230** Construction of the *palatium* lining*, exterior enclosure, and Aude Barbican.

**1240** Raimond Roger Trencavel's failure to regain the City; destruction of the market towns.

**1240-1245** Repairs to the exterior enclosure and erection of the Tour de la Vade; modifications to the interior enclosure, raising part of the château's domestic quarters.

**1248** Creation of the lower town.

**1269-circa 1322** Construction of Saint-Nazaire's gothic chevet and transept.

**1280-1287 (or later)** Repairs to the south corner and east front of the interior enclosure, construction of the Tours Narbonnaises and Tour du Trésau.

**1657** Transfer of the central royal administration to the lower town.

**1659** Treaty of the Pyrenees with the annexation of Roussillon; Carcassonne's loss of its role as the town closest to the Franco-Spanish border.

**1804** The City is struck off from the list of fortified towns.

**1851** Beginning of restorations.

**Circa 1910** Essential restorations completed.

**1997** UNESCO declares the City of Carcassonne a world heritage site.

# VISIT

*Following pages*

Top: Western front of the ramparts before restoration, O. Mestral photograph, 1851 (Paris, MAP/AP);

Bottom: Actual western front after Eugène Viollet-le-Duc's restoration.

The City functions both as monument and district of Carcassonne. Its trenches, ramparts, lists, towers, and Counts' château are state property, whilst streets and squares belong to the municipality. Houses are the property of individuals who use them as they wish, provided that, for all modifications or new construction, they respect directives from the Bâtiments de France's architect, a bureaucrat within the Ministry of Culture, Architecture and Heritage administration.

Visitors without a strict timetable may divide up their sojourn into several parts.

To begin, a promenade around the enclosure walls constitutes the best way to distinguish different construction phases and to become aware of the power of the fortification, by placing oneself in an assailant's position.

Next, a visit to the Counts' château and circuit around the curtain walls* of the interior enclosure allows one to better understand the City's history and to adopt the defenders' point of view.

A stroll through the streets leads the visitor to Saint-Nazaire Basilica, one of the most beautiful churches of the Midi. Several elegant edifices, the medieval fortified town plan, and an art of living typical of the Languedoc contribute to an unforgettable experience of the lower town.

## Enclosures

Four principal gates, orientated toward the cardinal points, give access to the City. The most frequently used is the **Porte Narbonnaise**[20-21], facing east toward Narbonne. The false drawbridge which allows traversing the trench is a late 19th-century invention. One must imagine in its

## Viollet-le-Duc and Carcassonne

A room in the château is consecrated to the work of Viollet-le-Duc (1814-1879) at Carcassonne. The architect's first mission involved the restoration of Saint-Nazaire Basilica, initiated in 1844. At the same time, he executed very precise measured drawings of existing sections of the City fortifications whilst accumulating observations on defence procedures and evolution of military architecture. At the request of the Service des Monuments historiques, he executed drawings restituting the state of fortifications at their peak in the early 14th century. The results of his observations and deductions reappeared in his *Dictionnaire raisonné de l'architecture française du XIe au XVIe siècle*. In 1858, he even published a small volume on the City.

From 1851, entrusted with the restoration of ramparts and towers, Viollet-le-Duc already thoroughly mastered his subject, but also knew how to manage the means at his disposal, the state of the monument, and its different construction periods. In the absence of an overall plan, he proceeded by degrees, according to credit allocated. Started up in 1853, construction was interrupted on several occasions. Responsibility for completion passed on to Émile Boeswillwald.

Eugène Viollet-le-Duc at age thirty, daguerreotype, 1845 (Neuilly, private collection).

Apart from a few exceptions, such as the Tour de la Porte Saint-Nazaire, which period photographs show in large part torn open and barely bypassing the first storey, ramparts and towers were collapsed only at their apex. Thus restorations were essentially carried out on the uppermost regions: crenellations*, roofs, certain vaulting. In other places, it was necessary to destroy parasitic constructions leaning against the ramparts which had transformed the lists into a veritable street and prevented an understanding of the role of the enclosures.

place a wooden bridge with a bascule section in order to create a void. The trench never contained water and encircled only half the City's perimetre. To the west, the sheer, rocky spur was such that it constituted a sufficient, natural obstacle.

After having taken the drawbridge, the visitor traverses diagonally southward —to the left with respect to the Tours Narbonnaises—to skim over the lists.

The first tower of the interior enclosure, called the **Tour Saint-Sernin**,[49] appears to be a Gallo-Roman construction (small bond with brick chaining), modified in the 13th century. The foundation mortar and large stone-block courses were unearthed during the levelling of the lists and restoration of defence wall underpinning. Two lateral bays were walled up; the enlarged, central window is in the Gothic style. In the 15th century, this tower served as the apse of the small Church of Saint-Sernin, destroyed during the Revolution.

The rectangular construction (which, a bit further, abuts the rampart) was not meant

Tour Saint-Sernin in the interior enclosure with its Gothic window from the former church.

for defensive purposes. It masks the **trauquet**[47] (little hole) giving access to a subterranean space which passes under the lists and gives out onto the trench at the foot of the Tour de la Peyre. Now walled up on the city side, this underground passage leads to a well, still supplied with water. Continuing along within the interior enclo-sure, one notices a few large stone frontage lines, obviously recycled, of unknown provenance.

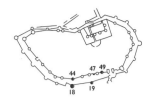

The **Tour de la Peyre**[19] and **Tour de la Vade**[18], the first two in the exterior enclo-sure, were constructed following damage inflicted during the 1240 siege. These towers are distinctly more powerful than the open, hollow* towers built earlier.

Tour de la Vade in the exterior enclosure with, in the foreground, the present cemetery occupying part of the old town of Saint-Michel destroyed in 1240.

The **Tour de la Vade**[18] (*vader* signifying 'to look') shifts one's view to a small, distant knoll now occupied by the City cemetery and which, before 1240, made up the extreme northern end of the town of Saint-Michel. The tower is a veritable free-standing donjon divided into five storeys, serviced by a staircase which spirals up within the rampart thickness. A well, fire-place, bread oven, and latrines assured the autonomy of the garrison. In the 14th and 15th centuries, a pole bearing a papegay

Pascal lamb representing the city coat of arms, on the keystone of Tour de la Vade.

Following pages

Viollet-le-Duc's restoration project for Porte Saint-Nazaire in the interior enclosure, pencil and gouache (Paris, MAP).

Postern and Tour de Balthazard, with the Tour de Davejean, Tour Saint-Laurent, Tour du Trauquet, Tour Saint-Sernin, and Tours Narbonnaises on the eastern front of the interior enclosure.

[popinjay], or brightly coloured, wooden bird, was attached to the top of the tower, serving as a target for the City's cross-bowmen.

Opposite the Tour de la Vade, the **Tour de Balthazard**[44] was the first on the interior enclosure not to incorporate any Late Empire features. Erected entirely under Philip the Bold, it was constructed in rusticated* bond with an almond-shaped profile—also called "*à bec*" [beak] or "*en éperon*" [spur]—meant to ward off attacks. Arrow slits* were placed in staggered rows from one storey to the next in such a way as to be able to multiply

# The lists

Originally the term *lists* designated palisades or picket fences behind which knights could take momentary refuge during tournaments. Subsequently, the term corresponded to the place of a tournament itself when it was demarcated by barriers. By extension, one gives the name 'lists' to all barriers or enclosed spaces.

At Carcassonne, lists are specifically that part of the terrain contained between the two enclosures. The natural profile of the hill, on a rather pronounced slope, was corrected in the 13th century to become a relatively flat terrain between the two ramparts. To the west where the slope is very steep, the lists are horizontal but at a price of being only of a very narrow width. To the north, the lists are much wider, but the profile of the slope could only partly be removed. To the east and south, where the natural difference of height is slight, the lists are wide and were easily flattened. In all cases, it was necessary to remove the earth at the base of the interior enclosure and carry it back against the inside face of the exterior enclosure. In disengaging the base of the interior enclosure, Gallo-Roman foundations and the ground on which they rested were often exposed. In this progressive,

Upper lists, south-east face, before destruction of the houses,
Jean-Eugène Durand photograph, 1891 (Paris, MAP/AP).

Upper lists today; left, Tour de la Peyre and Tour de la Vade in the exterior enclosure; right, Tour Saint-Sernin, Tour du Trauquet, Tour Saint-Laurent, Tour de Davejean, and Tour de Balthazard in the interior enclosure.

careful shoring-up, it was necessary to improve rampart underpinnings. A curious stratigraphy here follows. Under the Gallo-Roman foundations was found a type of smooth, rusticated bond of rather large dimensions characteristic of the 13th century. The late-Empire wall was held in a sandwich between this construction joint and the upper sections, the latter also restored. Existence of the lists is explained by the desire to bring together two successive lines of defence against assailants.

The exterior enclosure was always the lowest one so as not to create an obstruction to archers' and crossbowmen's shots from the interior enclosure. The exterior enclosure towers were most often hollowed out —wide open on the city side—in a way that they could not serve as refuge to the enemy had the first line of defence been captured. The lists provided an open zone between the two ramparts with limited possibilities for manoeuvring, exposing those who would have scaled the first enclosure to close fire from the defenders of the second enclosure. An exit in the lists to inflict torture on the first detachments who would have been able to reach their objective was eventually less risky than in the open country face to face with the main corps of enemy troops.

At the City, whilst lists were flat and wide, the central pavement and gutter recall that, at the end of the 18th century, they had become a veritable street bordered with houses. These the poorest Carcassonne citizens had built against the interior rampart and in the extension of the exterior enclosure during a period when the City fortifications no longer interested anyone. Restoration work consisted partially in clearing away these parasitic constructions.

shooting angles while not weakening masonry around the same vertical.

Alongside this tower, a postern* (situated approximately three metres below the level of the lists) represented one of the secondary egresses from the City. Another postern (at the base of the Tour de la Vade) leads to the trench.

More significant was the **Porte Saint-Nazaire**,[39] fitted into the **Tour** of the same name. Easily recognisable by its square plan, it assured southern access to the City. Orientation of the entry within the lists obliged the assailant to present his right flank, unprotected by the shield, to the crossbowmen posted behind the loopholes. A portcullis*, preceded by a machicolation*, and a heavy door blocked by a wood crosspiece made up the first series of obstacles. Then the assailant was forced to turn within a right angle to confront (on the city side) the same mechanism. This elbow-shaped passage, intended to impede manoeuvring a battering ram*, explains why a square plan was adopted. To avoid all dead angles, bartizans* were installed at the four corners of the tower summit, thus multiplying shooting angles.

By following along the promenade in the lists, one notes the very homogeneous,

Tour du Grand Burlas at the extreme south-west point of the exterior enclosure.

powerful, and manicured character of this section of the interior enclosure, totally reconstructed under Philip the Bold. At the extreme south-west point of the fortification, at the base of the **Tour du Grand Burlas**[12], remains of a Gallo-Roman tower were unearthed. One recognises the horse-shoe shape whose filled core appears to have tilted forward. This caving-in was probably provoked by Philip the Bold's architects when they had wanted to get rid of this portion of the late-Empire enclosure.

A staircase descends to a postern which allows passage outside the double line of defence. Calm, seldom frequented, and lined with vegetation, the path stretching along the exterior western-front enclosure offers extremely beautiful perspectives. Here the two enclosures are brought together in very close proximity to such an extent that the square-shaped **Tour de l'Évêque**[10] spans over them both. Short cuts multiplied as a result, allowing interruption of circulation within the lists. Church property stretched across the City's entire south-west corner. In 1280, Bishop Jean Gautier ceded a fringe of his own lands to facilitate reconstruction of the interior enclosure. In exchange he obtained

## The Inquisition at Carcassonne

Entrusted to the Dominicans, the Inquisition was a judicial body founded by Pope Gregory IX in 1231 to fight against heresy. Few in Carcassone were burned by the Inquisition, yet it avidly confiscated property of its victims. Above all, it rendered their life unbearable by a climate of permanent suspicion which weighed heavily on the local population.

In the earliest years of the 14th century, the Franciscan Bernard Délicieux, somewhat stirred up, and Élie Patrice, a lower-town resident who enjoyed great popularity, led a movement against the Inquisition. These two orators made an appeal to Philip the Fair, who first benevolently listened to them, but ended up by being antagonistic to their demands. They then proposed to the Infante of Aragon the delivery of Languedoc if he would get rid of the Inquisitors' land. The affair was discovered: the Infante received a thorough sounding from his father, the seneschal of Carcassonne had Élie Patrice and his accomplices captured, and Bernard Délicieux (who depended upon ecclesiastical justice) was emprisoned in a convent, and the city deprived for a time of its consulate.

As such, the Inquisition was responsible for one of Carcassonne's last political upheavals which put into question the issue of annexation of its territory to the royal domain.

Tour de l'Inquisition interior.

the right to have some handsome Gothic windows pierced through the upper portion of the ramparts to open up the episcopal enclosure toward the countryside, as well as to include enjoyment of the round tower, sometimes referred to as the **Tour de l'Inquisition**.[34] Its first storey was furnished with a beautiful chimneypiece; the ground floor served as solitary confinement, not for heretics but for clerics subjugated to ecclestistical law. The Inquisition prison, called the "*mur*" [wall] or "*mure*" [confine], was isolated within the countryside between the Aude River and City fortifications.

Our itinerary footpath next joins up with the rugged ascent to the **Porte d'Aude**,[32] the city's western entry. Slightly further, clinging to the extremely steep slopes of the hillock, two high ramparts loom, framing the ramp which links the château to the **Aude Barbican**.[60] This hefty, circular fortification was destroyed at the beginning of the 19th century and replaced by the small Church of Saint-Gimer, constructed by Viollet-le-Duc in 1854.

The city's interior enclosure subsequently merges with the château fortification, whose west gate opens onto a space which can be isolated from the rest of the lists by its traversing paths. At this point the covered path of the Aude Barbican terminates.

Continuing on within the lists, the visitor finally reaches the northern front. This is the section where the interior enclosure's appearance best recalls the Gallo-Roman fortification. The underpinning of ramparts

and towers is highly visible, but the profile of the hillock slope and breadth of the lists did not allow total levelling out of the latter. Protected by the **Tour du Moulin d'Avar,**[28] the **Avar Postern,**[29] with its rusticated block architrave, constitutes the sole late-Empire exit still practicable. From the northern City gate which opens on to the town of Saint-Vincent, under-pinning construction work destabilized the ramparts and towers. The **Tour de la Marquière**[25] leans to one side, the solid section of the **Tour du Vieulas**[24] inclines severely forward, whilst the upper storey was rebuilt upright and slightly recessed. The rampart was lined and reinforced with discharging arches.

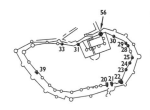

Beyond the **Tour du Moulin du Connétable,**[23] the interior enclosure recalls the very imposing appearance of Philip the Bold's constructions. It was erected in front of the Gallo-Roman enclosure modified under Louis IX. Razed to approximately mid-height by his royal architects and buried away under backfill, the tower was

---

### Tower names

Certain tower names are self-explanatory: **the Tours Narbonnaises,**[20-21] for example, are oriented toward Narbonne, and **Tour Saint-Nazaire**[39] located near the church of the same name.

Others allude to a function traditionally attributed to them, although authenticity is not always verifiable: **Tour de la Justice,**[31] **Tour de la Charpentière,**[30] perhaps once close to the royal carpentry, and **Tour de la Chapelle,**[56] integrated into the château's Sainte-Marie Chapel.

Other towers seem to correspond to a proper name. Is this in reference to a knight who had been in the guards during Trencavel's epoque or the first years of royal occupation, or rather, more prosaically, to Carcassonne citizens who appropriated the usage or constructed a few lean-to roofs in the late 18th or early 19th century?

Lastly, certain tower names are the result of courteous settlements amongst archeologists. When the thesis attributing the original interior enclosure construction to late-Empire Gallo-Romans prevailed over that of a Visigoth construction (very much in vogue in the 19th and early 20th centuries), the **Tour Wisigothe** regained its name **Tour du Four Saint-Nazaire,**[33] chosen by Carcassonne citizens after scholarly debates.

Upper-storey vaulted hall
in the Tour du Trésau.

Tour du Trésau and
Tour du Moulin du Connétable
within the interior enclosure.

unearthed down to its foundations a few years ago. On the town side, one is now able to see it set back from the breadth of the late 13th-century ramparts.

The two works built to defend the flank most easily accessible from the hill (where the city's principal entrance opens) are the most impressive within the fortified building ensemble. The **Tour du Trésau,**[22] whose name evokes a possible civic purpose in peace time, to assist the royal treasury, rises up five storeys of which two are magnificently vaulted. It is fitted with chimneypiece and latrines, with the rectangular addition descending along the exterior length of one of the sides acting as a drain. The run for guard rounds encircles the base of the roof; it is framed by watch turrets* and closed on the city-side by a Flemish gable end. As that of the Tours Narbonnaises,

Eugène Viollet-le-Duc's restitution of the Porte Narbonnaise's exterior facade, gouache drawing (Paris, MAP).

*Salle des Chevaliers* or Knights' Hall, second floor of the Porte Narbonnaise.

Tours de la Porte Narbonnaise within the interior enclosure.

the present flat-tiled roof is the result of a modification carried out by the first restorers, who had entirely covered the fortifications with slate during the 19th century. This alteration was justified by the royal architects' frequent use of flat tile, and by the reference (in a rare text concerning the City) to the size of tiles applied to circular building works.

The **Porte Narbonnaise**[20-21] consists of two twin towers linked by a châtelet*. Here one re-encounters a double system of closure—machicolation, portcullis, wooden folding doors, and, additionally, a break-back trap*. The ground-level arrow slits respond to an active notion of defence and to usage of a straight-shot crossbow. The north tower is furnished with an immense cistern, the south tower with a vast salting-tub. As for the Tour du Trésau and other large constructions of Philip the Bold, some niches equipped with stone banquettes were arranged to offer a small degree of comfort to the crossbowmen. On the upper storeys, a fireplace and bread oven assured the independence of this ensemble, conceived as an autonomous defence unit. The second storey displays concern for ceremonial pomp. Illuminated by five windows overlooking the city, the Salle de Chevaliers unites the three spaces of towers and châtelet.

# The Counts' château

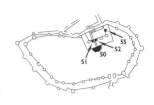

From the City, after having crossed through the semi-circular **East Barbican**,[50] the visitor first reaches the château, then the large trench straddled by a stone bridge, a crossing once likely traversed by a wooden bascule foot-bridge.

The château can be divided into three elements: fortified lining, court, and domestic quarters. The fortified enclosure was probably the first realization following upon the 1226 annexation of Carcassonne to the royal domain. Several options adopted here were taken up during the construction of the city enclosures. Thus, from the entry device, the twin **Tours de la Porte de l'Est**[51-52] frame a passage barred by a double system of machicolations with portcullis and folding wooden doors, all surmounted by a châtelet. There portcullis controls and machicolation openings are situated on two different storeys. A walk along the château's enclosing curtain walls allows us to see how the trestle or hoarding* gallery, here reconstituted on the east front section,

Section of the Counts' château's eastern front as seen from the first court interior known as the *"cour d'honneur"*[forecourt] with its trestle restoration.

Aerial view of the City's Counts' château.

Restored trestle gallery interior along a section of the eastern front of the château's forecourt.

assures the vertical flanking of the rampart. Its base *en fruit*, or slightly battered, obliged engineers to work precisely at the base of the floor ornamented with trestles. On the watch-tower* round, one becomes aware of numerous ruptures in levels which fragments the defence. Entering the tower rooms, the visitor appreciates the superb lateral flanking assured by the arrow slits. The first and second floors rest on flat-domed vaults, remarkably well dressed. Spiral staircases lead from one storey to another within the two corner towers; a system of trap doors and ladders is used for the other floors.

In **court**[a] (which one must imagine to have been much less spacious), two handsome plane trees now replace the feudal elm which once shaded it. The north sector was occupied by the Church of Sainte-Marie, built around 1150, whose substructures are still visible under the slightly raised slab which covers this part of the court. Access to these subterranean vestiges is made by a staircase fitted into the **Tour du Degré**.[55] Within this same basement are found the

Planted at the beginning of the 20th century, plane trees (replacing medieval elms) stand in the forecourt against the east facade of the Counts' château.

North section of the Counts' château, previously occupied by the Church of Sainte-Marie, with a rear view of the Tour du Degré.

remains of a beautiful Gallo-Roman house with intact wall bases, door thresholds, and mosaic floorings. Of the numerous light constructions abutting the interior enclosure and west-fronting buildings, that of the bakery (whose ovens are hollowed out within the wall thickness) have been unearthed.

From the court the visitor notices that a section of the dwellings has been raised. Traces of the *lauzes**, or heavy stone slate roofing, and that of the crenellated parapet are easily discernible in the superstructure. Diverse main sections of the domestic quarters were altered on multiple occasions, Romanesque openings (often no more than simple rectangular clefts) here run alongside Gothic bays and mullioned* windows. Certain sections were so disfigured that it was preferable to reconstruct them: on the north facade of the staircase leading to the Salle des Gardes (Guards' Room), the brick-filled timber framing* dates only from 1959. The ground floors are used as

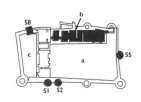

Rooms of the château transformed into a lapidary deposit: windows of the house known as "Gassalio" in the lower town, integrated into the Convent of the Cordeliers during the 19th century; keystone ornamented with a late 16th-century figure of Saint Louis from the Church of the Jacobins in the lower town; fleur-de-lys blazon of the Seneschalsy.

Vestiges of the great hall of the abode within the second court (called "Midi"), on the south side of the Counts' château.

service rooms or have yet to be furnished. On the first floor, visitors' reception takes place in the Guards' Room (although the original use of this room remains obscure, as for that matter all other rooms of the château). From the western defence of the château and interior enclosure of the city, a series of adjoining rooms form the west wing reuniting the triple function of the abode. The "*chambre ronde*" [circular room], perhaps thus named because of its semicircular vault, preserves some elements of its medieval decoration. On the springings of its vault, a mural painting evokes a combat between Franks and Saracens, possibly an allusion to expeditions to the Holy Land and Spain in which Bernard Aton Trencavel participated. Other rooms presently gather together an interesting **lapidary deposit**[b], which permits an evocation of Carcassonne and its regional history from the Roman period. There one

# Identification of construction phases

City fortifications appear to even the least well-informed eye as an extremely heterogeneous ensemble: not one tower is identical, and all ramparts present highly dissimilar features.

Adaptation to the terrain and functions of the constructions justify those differences, but also and foremost must be added a multitude of repairs, additions, and modifications witnessing evolution of a military architecture forever in search of greater efficiency.

Due to several characteristics specific to each period, dating (however approximative) is possible using every precaution that the rare text, each tower, and every rampart section inspires. Especial attention is given to different bond work.

**Late-Empire fortifications** (perhaps early 3rd century): within a cladding of small, rectangular bond (around 10 x 15cm) is inserted brick chain bond at various heights. Horseshoe-shaped towers are solid up to the first-floor level, fitted out with wide, semicircular bays emphasized by brick arch stones*. Re-use of 13th-century underpinnings often exposed foundations: mortar rolls, courses of coarse stone blocks for the walls, rectangular tower bases. Embattlement merlons* are solid, without loop-holes. Lastly, fluting tiles which now serve as roofing recall Gallo-Roman *tegulae* and *imbrices* because of their installation method.

**Twelfth-century buildings** use medium bond of quasi-square form, still modest in dimension. Vaults are barrel-vaulted or half-domed, and arrow slits small and slightly splayed toward the interior.

**Mid-13th-century royal constructions (Louis IX)** employ rectangular bond which take on much larger dimensions. The majority of vaults have intersecting ribs. Long arrow slits, well splayed toward the interior, sit on triangular bases.

**Late 13th-century projects (Philip the Bold)** are characterized by large-sized bond laid out in a clearly elongated rectangle. On the face of each stone remains a projecting portion called "bossage" or rustication. Towers are often *"en éperon"* or *"à bec"*, that is, in counterfort or beaked imitating the shape of a ships' prow. Very long and widely splayed toward the interior, arrow slits terminate with band irons.

To explain such particularities as brick chain or rustication, one must rely on hypotheses. Brick cordons perhaps allowed the recuperation of a flat level before mounting the next stone course. Rustication rendered assault ladders' support unstable, perhaps facilitating the shattering of stone cannon balls launched by war machines. It also might have been a means to convey an image of a more imposing fortification.

can see, amongst other objects, early Christian sarcophagi, Romanesque sculpture (a 12th-century ablutionary), funerary slabs, recumbent figures, and Gothic religious sculpture.

A **second court**ᶜ occupies the southern part of the château. The pier bases, highly visible corbels* in the ramparts, a chimney-piece, and window half-way up the south curtain wall all provide multiple indices of the existence of an extremely vast hall which covered practically the entire courtyard space from the 13th to 15th centuries. That court today remains dominated by the **Tour Pinte**,[58] both watch-tower and emblem of power.

The château visit generally includes a walk around the section of the interior enclosure curtain walls. The visitor may also penetrate into the tower interiors to better understand the position of the defence posted on the watch-tower round, and to admire exceptional views beyond.

# City streets,
# Saint-Nazaire Basilica

Within the City, examples of authentic medieval civic architecture are rare and of very average quality. One encounters a few 14th- and 15th-century half-timber* houses near the basilica and the château barbican, and several stone buildings near the Porte d'Aude (including the dwelling known as "of the Inquisition") on the Rue Notre-Dame and the Rue du Comte-Roger. On the Rue Saint-Jean, a rather pretty Renaissance construction awaits rehabilitation. As for the rest, a taste for the Middle Ages more or less successfully blends with commercial imperatives. Nonetheless, a promenade through the City streets does not lack charm, especially during the early morning or at nightfall when the shadowy lanes evoke a bit of their original mystery. **Saint-Nazaire Basilica**[61] alone merits a stop at Carcassonne, even if the City fortifications did not exist. The exterior is hardly seductive. The sandstone used

for construction and gables* is scaling off in numerous places, and the crenellation added by Viollet-le-Duc at the summit of the west side is questionable at the very least. By contrast, the interior volumes, sculpted decor, and stained glass windows are truly remarkable, and Viollet-le-Duc's restorations altogether skilful. The coexistence of two sections, Romanesque and Gothic, is evident, but the two styles complement rather than oppose each other. Of the Romanesque cathedral (whose construction terminated in 1096), only the nave and side aisles remain. Their narrow barrel-vaults buttress the pointed-barrel vault of the nave which, devoid of high windows, receives light only from the low

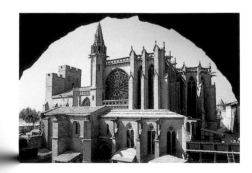

South transept arm and Gothic
chevet of Saint-Nazaire Basilica;
in the foreground,
Guillaume Radulphe's
mid-13th-century chapel.

windows of the side aisles and oculi perched high on the west facade. As a consequence, the Romanesque cathedral must have been rather sombre.

Carcassonne's annexation to the royal domain in 1226 made a force entry of art from the Île-de-France. Reconstruction work on the chevet and transept began in 1269. By this date, the Sainte-Chapelle in Paris had already been finished by

Romanesque nave of Saint-Nazaire Basilica looking west toward the organ case.

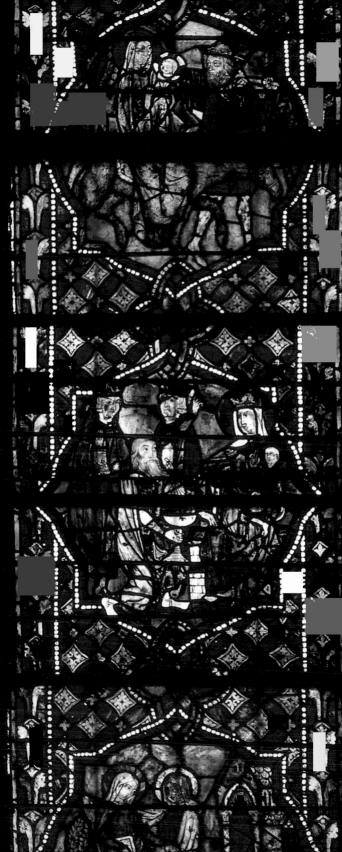

twenty-one years, and probably served as inspiration for the sculptural decor of Saint-Nazaire. Twenty-four sculptures are carved into the stone choir and transept piers, not set against the piers, as in the Sainte-Chapelle. The desire to bathe the choir and transept with a shimmering light translated into the quasi-disappearance, at a considerable height, of the absidal walls and transept chapels. The stained glass windows are all that separate the sanctuary from the exterior world. Several of these late 13th- and early 14th-century windows survive intact, relatively little altered by 19th-century restorations. The *Life of Christ* (from childhood to the Passion) is centred in the choir, with the *Lives of Apostles Peter and Paul* and *Lives of Saint-Nazaire and Saint-Celse* (patrons of the church) positioned on either side. In one of the north cross-brace transept chapels, the *Tree of Jesse* illustrating Christ's geneology is represented and, in the south cross-brace, the *Tree of Life,* a painted translation of the meditation on Christ's Passion written around the mid-13th century by the Franciscan theologian Saint Bonaventure. Two large rose windows illuminate the transept arms: the northern section, dominated by blues and reds, is consecrated to the Virgin; the southern section, lightened by paler blues, greens, and yellows, is dedicated to Christ. Transept vaults in the narrow side aisles and chapels are carried up to the same height. Thus the flying buttresses became superfluous on the exterior, replaced by rather thin buttresses to resist lateral pressures. By contrast, on the interior, the quite stout main piers received unequal lateral pressures. To render the ensemble immovably attached and stable, medieval architects were obliged to install a network of iron flying shores. As at Sainte-Chapelle, vaults and walls were painted. Few traces survive from this original decor. Saint-Nazaire remained the cathedral of Carcassonne until 1801. By then the City was no more than an impoverished, outlying neighbourhood that the bishop had long ago deserted for the lower town.

# Bastide Saint-Louis

The town is organised around the Place Carnot, embellished with a charming mid-18th-century fountain. The site is particularly picturesque during market days when regional farmers display their produce there. Created in the mid-13th century to accommodate inhabitants from the ancient City's market towns, the lower town retains its draughtsboard plan characteristic of walled towns in southwest France. In 1355 during the Hundred Years' War, Edward, Prince of Wales (known as the Black Prince because of the colour of his armour)

Place Carnot with its Baroque fountain.

Ancient bridge over
the Aude River linking
the lower town (left bank) with
the City (right bank) looking
toward its western front
and Counts' château.

easily took possession of it. The town was pillaged and set on fire, whereas the English troops did not dare attack the City. Reconstructed on a more restricted surface, the town was protected by wide trenches transformed into boulevards in the 18th century, and by a fortified enclosure of which a fragment remains visible on the Boulevard Barbès adjacent to the Cathedral of Saint-Michel.

From the 14th to 18th centuries, Carcassonne's prosperity depended upon fabric manufacture and trade, and often it was due to the cloth merchants that several fine *hôtel particuliers*, or private mansions, were constructed. **Hôtel de Rolland** remains the most elegant, built in the mid-18th century on the Rue Aimé-Ramond. It presently houses the city hall.

In traversing up and down the Rue Verdun and the Rue Aimé-Ramond, one would have encountered the principal and most remarkable civic buildings of the lower town. In 1803, Carcassonne's episcopal headquarters was transferred from Saint-Nazaire to the Church of Saint-Michel. The new cathedral inherited Saint-Nazaire's treasure-house: furniture, paintings, sacerdotal vestments, and silver (including chalices, patens, and reliquaries), constituting a collection worth viewing.

Devastated by a fire in 1849, the **Cathedral of Saint-Michel** was restored, if not largely reconstructed, by Viollet-le-Duc beginning in 1857. Erected in the early 14th century,

Western facade,
Cathedral of Saint-Michel.

Saint-Vincent's parish and neighbourhood.

its plan remains typical of Gothic churches in southern France: a wide nave with neither side aisles nor transept, a great apse, and two choir chapels forming a chevet, with open, lateral chapels between buttresses. Its vaulting dates only from the 18th century; the original church was covered with a timber framework carried by diaphragm arches.

Its construction beginning in 1308, the **Church of Saint-Vincent** offers the same type of plan but with an even larger nave. There again, the vaulting is late, with diaphragm arches supporting a timber framing.

The City and lower town are linked together by an **ancient bridge** built in the late 13th century. On the right bank of the Aude at the foot of the City slope, the **Trivalle Quarter**

developed. In the street of the same name, two buildings attract our attention: the so-called **"Montmorency House"**, a stone Renaissance building with corbelled out* half-timbering, and a magistrate's house, erected in 1602, in a predominantly medieval style.

Carcassonne is perhaps the only city which can boast of an ability to offer visitors two works inscribed on the UNESCO list of world monuments: the City and the Canal du Midi. In front of the train station, the canal locks affirm the popularity of boating along the waterway designed by Pierre Paul Riquet between 1668 and 1681. Four or five kilometres from Carcassonne, towards Bram, one can admire the beautiful perspective of locks near the hamlet of Herminis.

# Glossary

**Arch stone:** a wedged-shaped hewn stone inserted into the construction of an arch or vault.

**Arrow slit, arrow loop, or loop hole:** a slot within a rampart or fortification wall to accommodate shooting.

**Barbican:** a jutting structure destined to reinforce defences of a gate.

**Bartizan:** a small structure, such as a turret, projecting from a building and serving for lookout or defence.

**Battering ram:** a war machine composed of a beam terminated by a metal shape fashioned as a ram's head, used to knock down walls and gates of a besieged city.

**Bond:** the manner in which materials constituting the cladding of buildings are cut and arranged.

**Break-back trap:** an opening in a vault or ceiling of a covered passage through which projectiles could be launched on an assailant engaged within.

**Châtelet:** a small, fortified castle or fort to protect a passage (bridgehead, ford, road, or access to a fortified château).

**Corbel:** a projecting stone or piece of wood in a wall to support a beam, cornice, or arcature.

**Crenellation:** a combination of battlements and merlons on a defence wall.

**Curtain wall:** the section of a rampart between two towers or bastions.

**Gable:** a triangular ornamental pediment, often pierced, crowning lucarnes and windows, or archivolts of gateways or portals.

**Timber framing or half-timbering:** a frame wall or wood-frame construction in which voids are filled with light masonry.

**Hollowed out (tower):** a tower wide open on the side facing the town in a way so as not to be able to serve as refuge for a potential assailant.

**Jetty or corbelling:** a cantilevered construction on a wall plane supported by consoles or corbels.

**Lauze, or heavy stone slates:** a flat stone, either limestone or schistose, used as a roofing element in southern France.

**Lining:** the rampart enveloping a structure in order to reinforce it.

**Machicolation:** an opening for downward fire through the floor of a projecting structure, by extension a cantilevered defence gallery.

**Merlon:** set between two battlements, the open section of a parapet at the summit of a rampart.

**Mullion:** each of the jambs and cross bars of a bay dividing its opening into compartments.

**Portcullis:** a wood or iron sliding grille, armed with clout nails, manoeuvred from a storey above the principal gate of a fortress to block access.

**Postern:** a small, secret door pierced through a fortification rampart, often giving out onto the trench.

**Rustication:** a projection in rough or hewn stone forming a bulge on a wall plane.

**Trestle or hoarding:** an overhanging wooden gallery placed at the summit of a rampart by an openwork floor from which projectiles are cast onto the enemy.

**Watch-tower:** a small tower or tourelle at the summit of a tower for a lookout.

**Watch turret:** an overhanging look-out or watchman's shelter on a fortified enclosure or tower to ensure surveillance.

## Further reading

Guilaine, Jean, and Daniel, Fabre, eds. *L'Histoire de Carcassonne,* Toulouse, Privat, 1984.

Panouillé, Jean-Pierre. *Carcassonne. Le temps des sièges,* drawings by Jean-Claude Golvin, Paris, Presses du CNRS/Caisse nationale des monuments historiques et des sites, "Patrimoine au présent" collection, 1992.

*La Chanson de la croisade albigeoise,* text introduced by Eugène Martin-Chabot, adapted by Henri Gougaud, Paris, Le Livre de poche, "Lettres gothiques" collection, 1989.